Get Organized Today!

5 Simple Steps to Help You Get Organized Today and Improve Your Productivity Tomorrow

By K. Elizabeth

Table of Contents

Introduction

We've all thought it before: "I'll just do it tomorrow." It's such an innocent thought, yet it has the potential to bring quite dramatic results. Sure, we can easily—too easily—say, "I'll just do it tomorrow" as we sit looking at the pile of paperwork neatly stacked on our work desk an hour before closing time. But what about tomorrow? What happens when we receive yet another pile of paperwork tomorrow at the same time? Well, it looks like we'll now need to complete *two* piles of paperwork in a limited amount of time—yikes.

Putting off today's task for tomorrow can be quite a vicious cycle, one that overwhelms us, bogs us down, and oftentimes sparks the alluring thought of procrastination. And here's the thing—procrastination doesn't *just* happen at work. It happens in our very own homes as well—we tiptoe past the cluttered office down the hall that is in desperate need of extreme organization. We divert our eyes from our children's room—floors blanketed by dirty clothing, windows lined with empty food bowls, sheets, pillows, and blankets strewn across unmade beds. Sometimes we're simply *not* in the mood to tackle such organization-heavy endeavors. This, of course, is perfectly okay even once and a while, but not *every day*.

Sometimes we simply don't know where to start—organizing and improving productivity can be fickle, overwhelming tasks. So, we simply delay it as long as possible. Other times, we simply can't avoid our procrastinating personalities or our poor communication skills. It's just who we are. No matter what your situation is, however, you'll find some excellent resources and suggestions throughout the following chapters of this book. You'll discover simple, painless ways to organize your home *today*. You'll learn how to identify your procrastinating thoughts and how to push them aside so that you can find the motivation to tackle projects without dragging your feet. You'll learn how to prioritize at work and at home so that the most urgent tasks and projects get accomplished in beneficial, timely manners. You'll learn how to communicate effectively with others so that endeavors no longer get brushed aside for *later* dates. You'll also gain some familiarity with how to improve and maintain your attention span so that your complete and undivided concentration may be placed upon accomplishing your tasks promptly and efficiently. In short, you'll discover the key essentials for becoming organized and improving productivity *today*.

Chapter 1: Organize Your Home

"Cleaning your house while your kids are still growing is like shoveling the walk before it stops snowing."

-Phyllis Diller

Whether it's a matter of picking up a few things around the house or tackling the cluttered, disheveled, looks-like-a-tornado-blew-through-it room in your apartment, home organization all too often gets brushed aside for what we deem to be "more pressing matters." But let's face it: many of us will rationalize doing essentially *anything* else in order to avoid fixing the clutter around our home—we all of a sudden just *need* to read that book from the library before it's due. We just *need* to run to the store to pick up a few groceries. We just *need* to catch up on our favorite Monday night television programs.

But the truth is that we all *need* to clean and organize our home at some point. It's often a dreaded task, which is why we all too often brush it aside for tomorrow. The brutal truth is, though, that tomorrow we'll brush it aside for the next day, then the next, then the next. It's an innocently vicious cycle that we eventually need to break. And guess what? Today's the day you break it.

Big Difference, Quick Fix

No matter how neat you or your family members are, there *will* come a time when your home needs a bit of organization. Random objects casually tossed into the junk drawer need to be sifted through, pillow cases need to bc washed, desk drawers need to be cleared out, and living room bookshelves need to be dusted and reorganized. When we let these little things go, they build up—and quick. Luckily, there's an easy remedy to this problem. If you're short on time but your home needs some serious organizing, try:

- **Start Big**. We're often tempted to tackle the little places first when we organize—the kitchen junk drawer, our office desk, the misplaced objects on the living room shelves. The thing is, though, that you won't see much of a difference at first. Failure to see immediate results is certainly disheartening, and it'll more than likely deter you from proceeding. Instead, start with the biggest misplaced objects—clothing strewn across bedroom floors, empty dishes lining your children's windowsills, the rapidly growing pile of shoes in the closet. You'll immediately notice the results of your cleaning and organizing without breaking a sweat.

DIY Home Organization Projects

If you've got a bit of free time on your hands and enjoy working with your hands, then there's a whole world of DIY home organization projects out there for you to try. You might want to:

- **Organize your tight closet space:** Buy a set of 20 plastic, openable loops and a couple shirt hangers. Place the strap of a piece of clothing through each separate plastic loop, and fill the shirt hanger with your 20 loops (and therefore 20 pieces of clothing). (Great for small bedroom closets that are short on space!).

- **Organizing the shoe pile:** Purchase a light-weight, plastic, multi-drawer storage unit for each family member to throw their shoes in. It'll keep your shoe closet neat and clean, and it'll make your children's morning routine a lot smoother when they don't need to spend 10 minutes looking for the mysteriously missing other shoe. Let your kids get excited about this new organizer—encourage them to add stickers and decorate their personal drawers.

- **Recycled wall fixtures:** Turn old dresser drawer nobs into wall fixtures for holding bathrobes, towels, and children's jackets (great for small bedrooms, bathrooms, and closets).

- **Slim down your pantry:** Transfer spices, cereals, snacks, and finger foods into stackable storage containers to save room in your pantry.

- **Organize your dresser drawers:** Cut pieces from cardboard boxes and use them as dividers to separate your socks, belts, and undergarments that always seem to be mixed together in your dresser drawers.

- **Create corner space:** Learn to love corner shelves—you'll create extra space in every corner in which you add them.

- **Hallways into shelving space:** Take advantage of an underused hallway to add floor to ceiling shelfing.

- **Under the bed storage:** Stop by your local furniture store and purchase a cheap, tall, and skinny book case. Lay it on its side, slide it under your bed, and admire the organized, easy-to-reach, and still visually appealing storage space.

If you're interested in discovering more, be sure to check out:

- ❖ **Pinterest.com.** With a *free* account, you can search virtually anything with the click of a button. You'll want to use keywords such as "Home organization," "Home DIY projects," or "DIY Clutter-Free."

❖ **House Beautiful.** With its easily navigable layout, you'll quickly discover hundreds of simple yet fantastic ways to reduce household clutter, create storage space, renovate your home for low costs, and how to make tight areas have the allusion of space, to name a few.

Chapter 2: Avoid Procrastination

"Only put off until tomorrow what you are willing to die having left undone."

-Pablo Picasso

Balancing our chaotic work schedules, our children's afterschool activities, our social lives, our relationships with our partner or spouse, our physical health, and our own personal needs can become quite the juggling act—and a hard one at that. We all too often entertain the thought "I'll just do it tomorrow," but let's be honest for a second here. How well does this rationalization *really* work out?

We're busy people with hectic schedules, and that's perfectly fine. But when we don't stay on top of our busy schedules and our to-do lists, we fall behind. Perhaps worst of all, however, we procrastinate—a terribly crippling and unproductive action that has *never* done anyone any good in the long run. Why? Well, a habitual procrastinator often carries a negative reputation—one that infamous procrastinators probably aren't even aware of. Fortunately, there are a few simple remedies to this problem.

Thoughts of a Procrastinator

Sometimes it takes the form of the classic, nonchalant phrase, "I'll just do it tomorrow." On other occasions, it subtly invades our thoughts as we rationalize, "I'm too exhausted to produce quality work *today*, so I'll just put it off until I can approach it with a refreshed mind *tomorrow*." It's certainly a clever mindset, but it's also quite an unproductive one, too. For many of us, procrastination has gotten the best of us at some point in our lives, and for the unlucky few, procrastination gets the best of us almost every day. But no matter who you are—the conscientious and productive individual who only sometimes finds themselves swamped by the alluring thought of procrastination, or the lax, put-it-off-until-tomorrow individual whose struggle with procrastination is simply a part of their everyday routine—the following information will help. To begin, here are a few of the most common yet crippling thoughts of procrastinators (so that you can judge your own procrastination for yourself):

- **"Right now isn't the right time."** The truth is that it might never be the "right time." The busy individual might always have something else he or she could be doing instead, but this doesn't mean you shouldn't tackle the task at hand. In other words, you need to *find the time.*

- **"I don't have the right materials."** This can be a tricky thought to correct because you sometimes really *won't* have the right materials needed to start or complete a task. However, this doesn't mean you can stand there and twiddle your thumbs until the materials magically appear in front of you—this simply won't happen. Acknowledge what you're missing, then *do something about it.*

- **"I'm not in the mood."** Exhaustively long and stress-filled days happen, so this thought is perfectly natural to have. And you know what? It's okay to not be in the mood to complete a task. If the deadline isn't tomorrow and you're being responsible about it, you certainly *can* put off the task until you feel refreshed. But keep this in mind: this shouldn't be your default excuse with every task. If this thought creeps up often, you might be a habitual procrastinator.

- **"I work better under pressure."** Ek! This phrase is like hearing nails eerily and slowly scraping down a chalkboard. You might *think* you work better under pressure, but it's probably because it's the only way you *know* how to work. Think: do now, relax later.

Simple Ways to Eliminate Procrastination

No matter your personal procrastinating history, there are quite a few simple yet highly effective ways to manage or even eliminate your procrastinating tendencies. Here's how:

1.) Make a to-do list: Actually, perhaps a better title for this first step might be "Make a what-I'm-avoiding-list." Fixing a procrastination problem starts with an acknowledgement—of what you're not doing and why you're not doing it. So, write down the tasks you're avoiding and a quick explanation of why you're avoiding them. When you finish this, you'll have a brief but helpful list that clearly outlines what you *need* to focus on and what you need to do to in order to be successful.

2.) Approach it in steps: More often than not, procrastination stems from our confusion over where to begin. So, try breaking your task down into small, easily accomplishable steps. Doing so will make your task seem less daunting, but it'll also give you the allusion that you're not putting *all* of your time into accomplishing it. The feeling of accomplishing parts of your task will give you the right amount of motivation you need to complete the task's entirety, too.

3.) Establish specific deadlines: Deadlines are, in many cases, what causes procrastination in the first place—we dread and fear them. Yet, they're also a great way to resolve and prevent procrastination (as long as you strictly follow them). You'll want to set reasonable and attainable deadlines, and you'll want to set them often. So, draw up a chart that lists the steps you *will* complete and when you'll have each step completed by. Be as specific as possible. Here's an example of what this might look like:

Task Name	Duration	Start	Finish (due)
#1: Write	3 Days	3/1/16	3/3/16

Proposal			
#2: Prepare Proposal Presentation	2 Days	3/4/16	3/5/16
#3: Revise Proposal	2 Days	3/6/16	3/7/16
#4: Edit Proposal	2 Days	3/8/16	3/9/16
#5: Submit final proposal			3/11/16 by 5:00p.m

4.) Do it first thing in the morning: For many of us, the first sign of procrastinating thoughts crop up when we dread something. We dread the amount of time we think we'll need to put into our project. We dread the thought that despite our best efforts, our time and dedication might not even pay off. We might even dread the feeling of other tasks piling up as we work toward completing our current one. When we loathe or dread something so much, we all too often form excuses or rationalize away the guilt of putting off a task until tomorrow. Don't give yourself the opportunity to do this. Work towards completing your task first thing in the morning *before* you have time to develop creative excuses.

5.) Bribe yourself: Think: If I finish this *now,* I get to go out with friends for dinner and drinks *later* tonight.

6.) Visualize: This is a highly effective tool when it comes to accomplishing goals, so embrace it. Envision how productive and successful you'll feel when you complete the task at hand. Imagine what you'll treat yourself to when you've accomplished your goal. Let these moments of self-reflection and visualization fuel your motivation for completing the task.

Chapter 3: Prioritize...Everywhere

"I know that each of us has much to do.
Sometimes we feel overwhelmed by the tasks
we face. But if we keep our priorities in order,
we can accomplish all that we should."

-Joseph B. Wirthlin

The ability to prioritize is a highly valuable skill to have when organization, productivity, and deadlines beckon us. Without it, procrastination sets in, we fail to make deadlines, our ability to complete tasks falter, and our to-do lists grow exponentially. We get bogged down by the simple tasks that we really shouldn't get bogged down by. When we don't prioritize, we put off tasks until tomorrow, then the next day, then the next day, and so on.

If you haven't already discovered, the ability to prioritize comes in handy during a wide assortment of situations. Our ability to prioritize helps us succeed at work—we know what tasks to tackle first, we know what obstacles we need to overcome in order to move forward, and we understand what particular actions will lead to our highest degree of success. Yet, our ability to prioritize helps us keep our home and personal lives organized as well—we know what rooms need the most decluttering before the relatives visit for the weekend, we know what errands require the most attention, and we thrive when we're able to prioritize and balance our physical health with our hectic work schedules.

So, what should I prioritize?

Unfortunately, there's really no clear answer to this question. What you choose to set as main and minor priorities will depend upon your personal goals. For example, let's say you're working toward a promotion. In this situation, you'd want to prioritize the tasks at work that best allow you to exhibit your exceptional skills to your boss and demonstrate your ability to lead and work with others. Or, let's say you're a self-employed artist and want to have your work accepted into a national art gallery. In this situation, you'd want to prioritize your painting of portraits over your selling of portraits—the more paintings you have to offer the national art gallery, the higher your chances are of earning a spot. As you're hopefully beginning to see, exactly *what* you should prioritize doesn't have a clean-cut answer. However, the following suggestions are simple and helpful ways to help the prioritization process go smoother, no matter what your endeavors may be.

Task List at Work

Prioritizing at work is a must if you're seeking success, a rewarding career, and professional fulfillment. After all, exceptional prioritizing abilities are skills that, in part, allow you to successfully and flawlessly accomplish work-related tasks, capture the attention of your boss, gain the respect of your coworkers, and advance your career.

- **Start your day with a task list:** Before you so much as lift a finger at work, quickly jot down a list of tasks you'll need to complete throughout your day. (Do this as soon as you settle in and as soon as you figure out what needs to be done that day). After you have your list, rate each task in order of importance, 1 being the most pressing matter that should be tackled first. Carry and refer to your list throughout the day.

Follow up tips:

- **Adjust:** You might discover that new tasks crop up throughout the day. Don't simply add these next tasks to the bottom of the list. Review your list and find a spot for the new task among your initial tasks. Don't be afraid to cross out and revise the numbered ratings you gave each task at the start of your day.

- **Make your list simpler:** Sometimes rating each task in order of importance can be a difficult process, especially when your list seems to go on and on. If you find yourself in a similar situation, don't fret. Instead of assigning each task a specific numbered rating, simply divide your task list into two sections: "Urgent" and "Not Urgent." This method won't give you the same direction that rating each task does, but it's an excellent start.

Flexibility at Home

We talked about some great home organization and decluttering techniques in Chapter 1, but here are a few helpful suggestions that you should keep in mind as you prioritize the tasks you accomplish at home:

- **Avoid perfectionism:** Having a clean, organized home is a great priority, but it shouldn't be your *only* priority. You'll want to avoid a perfectionist approach to home organization as you set your home-related priorities. Allow room for the occasional moment of clutter so that you can accomplish other tasks as well—

helping your children with homework, spending time with your spouse, sitting down to read a good book, running household errands, etc.

- **Learn to be flexible:** This is an exceptional tidbit of advice for anyone with children, Things *will* get messy. They *will* get stained. They *will* be ruined. As you establish your priorities around the house, keep these things in mind. Having only one home-related priority—have a neat, organized, and clean household—absolutely won't work out with sticky hands, dirty clothes, and clumsy toddlers running around. Prioritize with flexibility to avoid disappointment and unnecessary frustrations.

Prioritizing For Everything Else

I know, I know. This is a rather broad topic. "Everything else" can refer to, well, everything else. Fortunately, here's a great tip that really does relate to prioritizing *everything else*:

- **Prioritize with logic and reason:** It's certainly a simple suggestion, but it's also quite an effective one at that. Prioritizing is an incredibly valuable skill that promotes our organization and self-improvement, but our prioritizing efforts falter when we aren't realistic. For example, let's say you're on a health kick and want to lose 20 pounds. You've prioritized your time at the gym, which is great, but when you get home from the gym, you indulge in your usual junk food habits. You haven't prioritized eating healthy. For anyone who is unfamiliar with losing weight, exercise and healthy eating go hand in hand. So, when you prioritize gym time but not healthy eating, your goal becomes harder to accomplish and perhaps even unattainable. So, spend some time thinking before you set your priorities in order. Be honest with yourself. You'll thank yourself later for it.

Chapter 4: Communication

"Communication—the human connection—is the key to personal and career success."

-Paul J. Meyer

If you live in a busy household, effective communication can be a hard thing to manage. The same goes for communication at work and communication in your relationships. It's such a crucial component of our everyday lives, yet we often struggle to keep the line of communication open. But here's the thing: when we *do* struggle to communicate effectively—whether it's the conveyance of our thoughts, ideas, or goals— the tasks we should accomplish today oftentimes turn into tasks that get brushed aside for tomorrow, next week, next month, or next year.

I'm sure many of us are able to see the benefits of effective communication in general. Yet, it's sometimes hard to understand how communication helps us better organize ourselves and prevent procrastination. So, let's approach this chapter with a specific topic in mind—group collaborations. I've chosen to use this example because it's one of the activities many of us encounter (in some form or another), and it's one that requires excellent communication skills.

Before we discover an excellent technique that helps foster effective communication and improves our organization and productivity, let me clarify something very quickly. We're going to talk about group collaborations for the rest of this chapter, but this can refer to a wide variety of things. For example, it might refer to:

- How the members of your household communicate and interact with one another.

- How you interact with your coworkers and supervisors in a professional setting or the work environment.

- How you work with others to complete tasks, accomplish objectives, and meet deadlines.

Verbal Role Assignments

Staying organized and remaining productive,—major elements that motivate us to complete tasks *today* and not *tomorrow*— are very much a group effort. A home can't stay clutter free if only one household members is dedicated to maintaining its organized state, and a group business proposal will never meet the submission deadline if one or more group members continually procrastinate. So, no matter what your objective is—an organized household or completing a professional task, for example—communication in group collaborations is a must.

But like we discovered in earlier chapters, broad, overwhelming goals are what cause us to procrastinate, prioritize incorrectly, and push aside today's task until tomorrow. Fortunately, there's a fairly simple fix to this. You'll want to:

- **Assign each member of your group a different, productive role.**

That's the main gist, really. So, let's say that you have a disorganized, cluttered household. If just *you* were to be in charge of maintaining your home's organized and neat appearance, you'd probably feel overwhelmed. The chores you *should* do today after work—vacuuming, cleaning the closet, and dusting—might get pushed aside until tomorrow when you return home from an exhaustively long day at the office. But when you assign each of these tasks to each family member—you vacuum, your spouse cleans the closet, your son dusts—the original task becomes a series of small, accomplishable tasks. All chores are completed *today*, and in a very short amount of time, too.

The same idea might apply to group collaborations in the work place. Instead of setting up weekly outside-of-work meetings to work on a business proposal, you could assign each team member their on task to work on independently. One person generates ideas, two coworkers evaluate those ideas separately, one coworker serves as a mediator when confrontations or disagreements arise, you edit and revise the final written project proposal, and another coworker presents your group's business proposal during the business meeting. Everyone has *one* reasonably small task to complete by a set deadline, so procrastination is much easier to avoid. Assigning everyone their own task means things get done quickly and efficiently without all the added stress.

Chapter 5: Attention, Attention!

"The average attention span of an adult human is...wait, what was I saying?"

-Anonymous

Let's face it: our attention spans falter. All too many of us are guilty of setting aside an hour of our time to completing a certain task, but, within a matter of minutes, find ourselves mindlessly scrolling through social media posts on our phones or wondering off to complete an altogether different task. We may have the most genuine intention to tackle the cluttered, disorganized state of our office drawer, yet an hour later we've lost all motivation. We might cozy up in our favorite chair to read the book we've been dying to read for months, yet 30 minutes later we find ourselves searching for more entertaining or productive tasks to complete around the house. Attention is a fickle thing. We oftentimes set our minds to completing a certain task, yet find our attention wondering off or completed departed within a matter of minutes. And by the way, for those curious about the quote at the beginning of the chapter: recent studies suggest that the average attention span of a human adult is 8 seconds. 8 seconds! That means a goldfish— who has a 9 second attention span—can pay attention to something longer than most of us.

Maintaining our attention is vital. Without it, tasks get brushed aside until later dates. Projects are started but never finished. Activities that should only take 1 day turn into long-term projects that take weeks. Loss of attention creates disorganization. It creates task and projects that take far longer than they ordinarily should. It fosters procrastination.

Fortunately, many of these things can be avoided, and without much of a hassle, too. The following suggestions will help you improve and expand your attention span, which in turn will help you maintain a more organized and productive life. Your newly revamped attention will help you keep your home organized and will improve your ability to concentrate for longer periods of time at work. It's a win-win situation, really.

Quick Attention-Improving Tips

Attention is crucial in terms of our success and productivity, but it doesn't take much to improve it, fortunately.

- **Ditch coffee for exercise:** Sure, your caffeinated coffee *might* give you the energy needed to complete important tasks at hand and remain focused, but what happens when the caffeine in your system dissipates? Relying on coffee throughout your day is a quick fix, but it's certainly not the *best* fix. So, ditch your daily coffee for exercise. Study after study has shown just how beneficial physical exercise is for both the body and the mind. Essentially, physical exercise releases chemicals throughout our bodies that promote learning, memory, and, more importantly, concentration. So, if you're able to, use part of your lunch break to take a quick stroll down the road. Wake your body up. Give your brain the opportunity to refresh itself so that it can return to work with a clear, refreshed perspective.

- **Drink, drink, drink:** Water, that is. A 2012 study published in the *Journal of Nutrition* found that simple dehydration—simply not drinking enough water per day—can affect our attention-span. After all, our bodies are made up of 60% water, so you can see why it's important to stay hydrated throughout the day. Although the "drink 8 cups of water a day" theory has recently been debunked, you'll want to drink somewhere near this amount still. Actually, some studies now suggest women should drink about 9 cups of water per day, and men about 12.

- **Reduce distractions:** With today's technology, it's actually hard *not to* get distracted. We're constantly checking our emails, scrolling through our phones, and video calling long distance friends and family. Although the connectivity modern technology offers is great, it's also quite a powerful source of distraction. Just think about it: how many times has the simple chime, beep, or vibration of your idle cell phone next to you made you immediately stop what you were doing and pick it up? Yes, we're *all* guilty of doing this. Fortunately, there's a simple remedy—turn your phone on silent and place it facedown. Temporarily forget about it. Tackle the task at hand, but allow yourself a 5 minute phone-check every hour. Compromise with yourself until you're able to build up a resistance to constant phone-checking.

Maintaining Your Attention

So, you're exercising, drinking water, and reducing distractions. Now what? Well, you'll hopefully notice at least a slight improvement in your attention span, if not a noticeable one. But there's the thing: once you've improved your attention, you'll want to maintain it, too. Here's how:

- **Take frequent breaks:** Our brains tend to become fuzzy and muddled when we look at or do something for extended periods of time without pause. Actually, simply reading a book for more than 30 minutes can cause our attention to wane. To avoid this—and to allow your brain to refresh itself occasionally—take breaks. How frequent you'll want to take a break will depend on you and your personal attention span, but for most, a 10 minute break every hour proves to be a simple yet highly effective method to prevent waning attention spans. What you do during your *brief* break is up to you, but you don't want to do anything too crazy. Walking around, grabbing a quick snack to eat, stretching, and using the bathroom are all preferable break activities. You *don't* want to start a new project, watch TV, or settle down with any long-term activities during your short break—that's how you **lose** your attention!

- **Learn to love memorization activities:** It's a rather simple method, but it can be quite effective if you make memorization exercises, activities, and puzzles a part of your daily routine. Memorization, of course, requires our utmost attention and concentration, so it's a natural attention strengthener. It might help to think of our attention span as a muscle—it needs constant exercise in order to maintain itself. So, try memorizing a favorite poem or look up song lyrics by your favorite musician. Do your best to memorize the words in one sitting, and in as little time as possible. As your attention span increases, you should also find that your ability to memorize poems and song lyrics improves as well. It's a nice and simple way to see noticeable progress.

Conclusion

Life can get messy sometimes—literally and metaphorically. Our homes, especially with young children running around, can quickly become disorganized, cluttered, and in need of some desperate cleaning. Our productivity at work crumbles when we procrastinate, when we fail to prioritize, and when our attention aimlessly wonders off to unproductive thoughts. When it comes to our homes, our careers, and our personal lives, we all too often give in to the alluring tendency to brush aside today's tasks for tomorrow. We rationalize that tomorrow will be a more productive day. We convince ourselves that we'll tackle our pressing tasks tomorrow. We tell ourselves that today just simply isn't the right day.

This book has, hopefully, helped you discover ways in which to avoid the tempting thought of *doing* tomorrow. You've discovered simple ways to declutter, organize, and clean your home *today* in Chapter 1. You've learned how to identify the onset of procrastination and how to eliminate those pesky tendencies to put off today's activities for another time in Chapter 2. In Chapter 3 we discussed some helpful suggestions to keep in mind as you prioritize at work, at home, and for everything else you may encounter throughout your day. Chapter 4 introduced a great communication tool to employ, one that will improve group communication and will help you get things done quickly and effectively (so you can completely avoid the temptation of delaying things until tomorrow). You've also discovered a few simple yet proven ways in which you can improve and maintain your attention span in little to no time—a helpful tool that will let you complete tasks *now*, not later.

Yet, there's one more step that you need to do now: give these a try! Set aside some time to incorporate these simple techniques as you organize your home, work toward controlling your procrastinating tendencies, prioritize in all the environments you inhabit on a daily basis, communicate effectively with groups in order to accomplish tasks quickly, and improve and expand your attention span. So get to it—organize your life *today*.

....

www.ingramcontent.com/pod-product-compliance
Lightning Source LLC
Chambersburg PA
CBHW070410190526
45169CB00003B/1191